Strong Trucks

Written by Sarah Snashall

Collins

Strong trucks do all sorts of strong jobs.

digger

forklift truck

tipper

stunt truck

dumper truck

This stunt truck has deep grips to stop skids.

They smash scrap cars and bump up ramps.

The hammer on this truck splits rocks from the cliff.

The biggest dumper trucks shift the biggest rocks.

The digger digs a trench.

boom

stick

bucket

Next, a tipper truck tips in the grit.

The long arm swings and smashes.

The forklift truck brings a stack
of bricks.

At the scrapyard, magnets lift bits of cars.

The truck drops the scrap into the crusher.

Trucks

 Review: After reading

Use your assessment from hearing the children read to choose any GPCs, words or tricky words that need additional practice.

Read 1: Decoding

- Practise reading words that contain adjacent consonants. Encourage the children to sound out and blend the following:

  ramps   brings   cliff   swings   splits   trench

- Focus on double-syllable words. Check the children include all the sounds, for example check they do not miss "l" in **forklift**.

  bucket   forklift   dumper   magnets   scrapyard

Read 2: Prosody

- Model reading each page with expression to the children.
- After you have read each page, ask the children to have a go at reading with expression.
- Encourage children to emphasise words that show each truck's strength.

Read 3: Comprehension

- Turn to pages 14 and 15 and use the pictures to name and describe the trucks, and explain what they do.
- For every question ask the children how they know the answer. Ask:
  - On page 5, is crushing the cars a waste of money? (e.g. *no because they are scrap*)
  - On pages 6 to 7, why do you think the rock is split before it is moved? (e.g. *so that it can be taken away more easily*)
  - What opposite activities are happening on pages 10 to 11? (e.g. *page 10 shows a house being destroyed; page 11 shows bricks to build something new*)
- Discuss which truck the children thinks is the strongest, and why.